Sebra, Richard
Nevada

CORE LIBRARY OF US STATES

NEVADA

BY RICHARD SEBRA

CONTENT CONSULTANT
Joanne Goodwin, PhD
Professor of History
University of Nevada, Las Vegas

Core Library

An Imprint of Abdo Publishing
abdobooks.com

abdobooks.com

Published by Abdo Publishing, a division of ABDO, PO Box 398166, Minneapolis, Minnesota 55439. Copyright © 2023 by Abdo Consulting Group, Inc. International copyrights reserved in all countries. No part of this book may be reproduced in any form without written permission from the publisher. Core Library™ is a trademark and logo of Abdo Publishing.

Printed in the United States of America, North Mankato, Minnesota.
052022
092022

Cover Photo: Shutterstock Images
Interior Photos: Randy Andy/Shutterstock Images, 4–5; Red Line Editorial, 7 (Nevada), 7 (USA); Arlene Waller/Shutterstock Images, 10–11, 20–21, 45; Davis Ladd/iStockphoto, 12; Shutterstock Images, 17 (flag), 25; Georgia Evans/Shutterstock Images, 17 (sheep); Double Brow Imagery/Shutterstock Images, 17 (bird); Wirestock Creators/Shutterstock Images, 17 (flower); John Andrus/Shutterstock Images, 17 (tortoise); iStockphoto, 18, 23, 33, 43; Neil Lockhart/iStockphoto, 28–29; Steve Marcus/Las Vegas Sun/AP Images, 30; Kobby Dagan/Shutterstock Images, 34–35, 37; John Locher/AP Images, 39

Editor: Angela Lim
Series Designer: Joshua Olson

Library of Congress Control Number: 2021951403

Publisher's Cataloging-in-Publication Data

Names: Sebra, Richard, author.
Title: Nevada / by Richard Sebra
Description: Minneapolis, Minnesota : Abdo Publishing, 2023 | Series: Core library of US states | Includes online resources and index.
Identifiers: ISBN 9781532197697 (lib. bdg.) | ISBN 9781098270452 (ebook)
Subjects: LCSH: U.S. states--Juvenile literature. | Western States (U.S.)--Juvenile literature. | Nevada--History--Juvenile literature. | Physical geography--United States--Juvenile literature.
Classification: DDC 979.3--dc23

Population demographics broken down by race and ethnicity come from the 2019 census estimate. Population totals come from the 2020 census.

CONTENTS

CHAPTER ONE
The Silver State 4

CHAPTER TWO
History of Nevada 10

CHAPTER THREE
Geography and Climate 20

CHAPTER FOUR
Resources and Economy 28

CHAPTER FIVE
People and Places 34

Important Dates........................ 42

Stop and Think......................... 44

Glossary................................... 46

Online Resources...................... 47

Learn More 47

Index 48

About the Author...................... 48

CHAPTER ONE

THE SILVER STATE

Neon lights brighten the sky above Las Vegas, Nevada. The city's signs advertise some of the world's most famous entertainers. People from all over the world come to the City of Lights. But a different gleaming attraction first brought people to Nevada 150 years ago.

Nevada is known as the Silver State. The discovery of silver in Nevada in 1859 inspired thousands of people to move to the West and try to strike it rich. Nevada was not a state

Many famous hotels and casinos line the Las Vegas Strip.

NEVADA? NEVAHDA?

Nevada is a Spanish word. The Spanish pronunciation is ney-VAH-duh. But Nevadans pronounce it neh-VA-duh, with a shorter *a* sound that sounds like the *a* in the word *trap*. Even though it may not be proper Spanish, the local pronunciation is a form of state pride. The state even used to offer license plates with an accent mark over the first *a* to signal the proper pronunciation.

then and had only a few small towns. It started to grow quickly. The territory became a state during the American Civil War (1861–1865). That gave it the alternate nickname Battle-Born State.

ABOUT NEVADA

Nevada borders five states. Oregon and Idaho make its northern border. Utah and Arizona lie east of the state. California is to the west.

Today most Nevadans live in Las Vegas. It attracts risk-takers and tourists looking to gamble. But Nevada is more than just one city. Reno is another

MAP OF NEVADA

Many of Nevada's biggest cities are located near water sources. Why do you think the area was developed this way?

PERSPECTIVES
DARK SKIES

Away from Las Vegas, Nevadans can take advantage of protected "dark sky" places. These areas are far away from city lights, allowing visitors to clearly see the stars. In 2021 Nevada had two official dark sky places. They were Great Basin National Park in eastern Nevada and the Massacre Rim Wilderness Area in the northwest. Protecting dark skies brings stargazers and other tourists to natural areas of Nevada. Marcia Hurd is the president of the Lincoln County Tourism Authority. She wrote, "Living in an area where you can clearly see the Milky Way just by stepping out your backdoor is something that everyone should have the opportunity to experience."

popular destination. Big deserts, tall mountains, low valleys, and famous lakes attract tourists. The state also has a diverse population.

Nevada can be a hard place to live. Its hot deserts don't offer much relief. But Nevadans find plenty to love about their home state.

STRAIGHT TO THE
SOURCE

On September 28, 2019, Nevada celebrated its third annual Public Lands Day. This day was created to honor Nevada's cultural and historic outdoor spaces. During the celebration congressperson Susie Lee said:

> *The thing I cherish the most about Nevada is our wide-open spaces. We are blessed with incredible public lands—from Red Rock, to Sloan Canyon, to Spirit Mountain. They encapsulate our history, our vitality, our health, and our happiness. I love starting my day with hikes or bike rides along our Valley's landscapes, and I truly can't imagine my life without the opportunity to do those things in my backyard. For our environment, community, and the health of the entire country, we need to continue fighting to conserve America's public lands.*

Source: "Governor Steve Sisolak Marks 3rd Nevada Public Lands Day with a Signed Proclamation." *Battle Born Progress*, 28 Sept. 2019, battlebornprogress.org. Accessed 16 Mar. 2021.

CONSIDER YOUR AUDIENCE

Adapt this passage for a different audience, such as your principal or friends. Write a blog post conveying this same information for the new audience. How does your post differ from the original text and why?

CHAPTER TWO

HISTORY OF NEVADA

Humans have lived in Nevada for more than 20,000 years. These early peoples are called Paleo-Indians. They were hunters and gatherers who traveled around the Great Basin region of the state.

Over time the Paleo-Indians formed American Indian nations that are still recognized today. These include the Paiute, Shoshone, and Wašiw. These nations are made of individual tribes that have their

Many early peoples who lived in what is now Nevada traveled throughout the Great Basin area.

Lake Tahoe's clear, blue waters attract many tourists.

own unique cultures. The US government recognizes 19 American Indian nations in Nevada today.

The Paiutes include the Southern Paiutes and the Northern Paiutes, which both have multiple tribes. The Tudinu were ancestors to the Las Vegas Paiute Tribe of the Southern Paiutes. *Tudinu* translates to "desert people." Some Northern Paiutes settled around Pyramid Lake, where they were able to fish.

The Western Shoshone lived in central Nevada. The land was rich in wildlife. It was home to many fish and small mammals, and seeds and other plants grew well there. The Western Shoshone generally lived in small family groups. They sometimes worked with other Western Shoshone families while hunting.

The Wašiw lived around what is now Lake Tahoe, which is still an important cultural location for the Wašiw today. The lake was also an important source of food and medicine. *Tahoe* comes from the Wašiw word *da ow*, which means "the lake." During the winter the Wašiw traveled to the valleys of the Sierra Nevada, where it was warmer.

The first European to visit Nevada was Francisco Garces of Spain. He traveled to the area in the 1770s to spread Catholicism. It was Spanish explorers that named the Sierra Nevada mountain range in the western part of the state. *Nevada* is a Spanish word that means "snowcapped."

PERSPECTIVES
SARAH WINNEMUCCA

Sarah Winnemucca was a Northern Paiute American Indian. She was born near Nevada's Humboldt Lake in 1844. Nevada was still decades away from becoming a US state. Winnemucca's Paiute community was its own nation. Winnemucca published her autobiography in 1883. It was the first known autobiography from an American Indian woman. It told the history of her people as they lost their homelands to white settlers. Winnemucca later became an activist for American Indian rights. She traveled the country giving talks about the experiences of her people.

Despite the presence of American Indian peoples, the explorers claimed the land for Spain. The Nevada area remained a part of Spain into the 1800s. Control then passed to Mexico in 1821. The Old Spanish Trail was a trade route that ran through the state. This brought a lot of new settlers to the region. In addition, followers of the Church of Jesus Christ of Latter-day Saints settled in Nevada in the 1850s.

STATEHOOD

Silver was discovered in Nevada in 1859. Many settlers rushed into the area. This new population of people had a negative effect on American Indian peoples. Settlers took land and resources away from them. This sometimes led to violent conflict. Throughout the late 1800s, the US government forced American Indians off their homelands and onto reservations.

Despite the silver rush, Nevada maintained a relatively small population into the 1860s. But President Abraham Lincoln believed Nevada could help the North during the Civil War. Its silver could boost the North's economy. Despite having one-fifth the population needed to become a state, Nevada was admitted as the thirty-sixth state in 1864.

Nevada's government has three branches. The executive branch is led by a governor. The legislative branch has two houses of congress. There is the Senate, which is the higher house. In Nevada, the lower house is called the Assembly. And there is a judicial branch led by the state Supreme Court.

When Nevada first became a state, only white men could vote. The Fifteenth Amendment was added to the US Constitution in 1870. This gave Black men the right to vote nationwide. However, women were still unable to vote.

In the 1910s, women in Nevada began leading the charge for the right to vote. On November 3, 1914, a vote was taken to determine whether Nevada women would be granted this right.

CIVIL RIGHTS IN NEVADA

Throughout Nevada in the mid-1900s, Black people were treated much differently than white people. They did not have the same access to jobs and were not allowed into some businesses. For example, Black performers could not stay in the hotels where they did their shows. The US government passed the Civil Rights Act in 1964 that banned discrimination due to race. In 1971 Las Vegas worked with the federal government to end racial discrimination in its businesses.

NEVADA
QUICK FACTS

Many of Nevada's state animals and plants are found in the mountains and deserts. How does this help you understand Nevada's geography?

Abbreviation: NV
Nickname: The Silver State
Motto: All for our country
Date of statehood: October 31, 1864
Capital: Carson City
Population: 3,104,614
Area: 110,572 square miles (286,380 sq km)

STATE SYMBOLS

State animal
Desert bighorn sheep

State flower
Sagebrush

State bird
Mountain bluebird

State reptile
Desert tortoise

The Hoover Dam provides electricity for approximately 1.3 million people in the southwestern United States.

The vote passed, and women in Nevada cast their first ballots in the state's 1915 elections. It wasn't until 1920 that this right was granted to women throughout the United States.

After gambling was legalized in Nevada in 1931, a lot of money was brought into the state. Gambling helped build the economies of Las Vegas and other cities around the state. Reno turned into a gambling and entertainment destination as well.

Construction began on the Hoover Dam on June 6, 1933. It is located on the Colorado River and straddles Nevada and Arizona. It was built to protect the area from floods and to provide water for farmers. The dam created Lake Mead, which has the most water of any US reservoir. The Hoover Dam uses the flow of water to generate electricity. It is one of the largest hydroelectric plants in the country.

Over time Nevada became one of the fastest-growing states in the country. Its population first topped 3 million in 2018. And the state continues to attract tourists from all over the world.

EXPLORE ONLINE

Chapter Two talks about Nevada's early history. The article at the website below goes into more depth on this topic. Does the article answer any of the questions you had about the first peoples living in Nevada?

NEVADA HISTORY & HERITAGE

abdocorelibrary.com/nevada

CHAPTER THREE

GEOGRAPHY AND CLIMATE

Many people think of Nevada as a hot, flat desert. Most of Nevada does consist of one big desert basin. But it also has forests, lakes, and snowy mountain peaks.

Nevada is part of the Basin and Range region of North America. The Great Basin covers most of Nevada. It is a large desert region. It contains mountains and few natural bodies of water. Nevada has more than 300 mountain ranges, the most of any state.

People can enjoy a scenic drive around Wheeler Peak in Great Basin National Park.

The Sierra Nevada range in the west forms part of Nevada's border with California. It is also home to Lake Tahoe, which is the largest mountain lake in the United States.

The Great Basin has hot, dry summers and cool, dry winters. High elevations get snow. Boundary Peak is the state's highest natural point, with an elevation of 13,140 feet (4,005 m). Nevada's lowest point is the Colorado River, which runs along the state's southern border. It is just 480 feet (146 m) above sea level. The wide

PERSPECTIVES

STATE PARKS

State and national parks are protected areas of land. Only a few people, such as David Low, get to live there. Low is a park ranger in Spring Mountain Ranch State Park. He is originally from the Midwest but was drawn to the beautiful landscape of Nevada. His daily duties include opening up the park for visitors and leading educational programs. "You can completely forget that you're 25 miles (40 km) from the Las Vegas Strip when you come up here," Low said. "We're kind of a hidden gem."

A bristlecone pine tree, one of Nevada's state trees, is able to survive in cold, dry places.

range of elevations in the state means that Nevada can experience extreme temperatures. Nevada's highest recorded temperature was set in Laughlin, one of Nevada's lowest points, on July 29, 1994. The temperature reached 125 degrees Fahrenheit (52°C).

The lowest temperature recorded in Nevada was set approximately 500 miles (805 km) north of Laughlin.

On January 8, 1937, the temperature in San Jacinto was −50 degrees Fahrenheit (−46°C). San Jacinto sits 5,200 feet (1,585 m) above sea level.

Nevada is the driest state in the country. It averages just over 10 inches (25 cm) of rain per year. Southern Nevada includes part of the Mojave Desert. That's where Las Vegas is located. The Mojave is the driest desert in North America.

Nevada is already very hot. Climate change threatens to make it even hotter and drier. This increases the chance of wildfires, which could destroy animal habitats and pollute the air. Wildfires have other lasting effects, like property damage to homes and businesses.

In addition, climate change further limits the water available in the state. In 2020 Nevada saw a record dry streak. The water level of the Colorado River has also dropped in recent years. Las Vegas gets most of its drinking water from the Colorado River. Because of the

A rattlesnake's colors help it blend in with its desert surroundings.

low water levels, a Nevada government agency had to build additional intake sources at Lake Mead to provide water for Las Vegas residents. It also constructed a pumping station to help access more water. This station was completed in 2020.

PLANTS AND ANIMALS

Many plants and animals cannot survive in such hot conditions. But some have adaptations that allow them to thrive in deserts. Desert creatures that live in Nevada include Gila (pronounced HEE-lah) monsters and rattlesnakes. Gila monsters burrow underground to seek cooler temperatures. Rattlesnakes also find shade during the day. When it rains, they collect water on their backs. They save the water to drink later.

Desert plants such as prickly pear cacti are common too. Nevada has more than 30 species of cacti. The state flower, sagebrush, grows throughout the desert.

Pyramid Lake is one of the largest lakes in Nevada. It is home to many fish species. The cui-ui (pronounced KWEE-wee) fish is an ancient species that has lived on Earth for more than 2 million years. This species can be found only in Pyramid Lake. The Lahontan

BRISTLECONE PINE

Many people think of cacti when they think of the desert. But one of Nevada's state trees grows in the dry mountains. The bristlecone pine is one of the longest-living trees in the world. Some are more than 4,000 years old. They can survive at high elevations and in cold conditions. If one of a tree's roots dies, the sections above that root can stay alive. The trees grow very slowly. On average, their trunks thicken only 1 inch (2.5 cm) every 100 years.

cutthroat trout also lives there. This state fish has attracted many fishers to Pyramid Lake.

Different plants and animals live in the mountains. Nevada's state animal, the desert bighorn sheep, lives on dry, rocky mountains. The sheep can use its horns to break open cacti. Black bears also live in the mountains. The single-leaf piñon is one of Nevada's state trees. Like other plants found in the state, the single-leaf piñon is able to survive with little water.

FURTHER EVIDENCE

Chapter Three discusses some of the effects of climate change on Nevada. What was one of these main points? What evidence is included to support this point? Read the article at the website below. Does the information on the website support the main point of the chapter? Does it present new evidence?

CLIMATE CHANGE
abdocorelibrary.com/nevada

CHAPTER FOUR

RESOURCES AND ECONOMY

Nevada's population grew throughout the 1860s. The mining industry attracted people hoping to strike it rich. Mining peaked in 1878, when the state put out $36 million worth of silver. That would be worth nearly $1 billion today. Silver was the major resource mined in the state. But gold and copper were also plentiful. New towns popped up throughout the region.

But the mining industry could not maintain the state's economic growth. The Great

Many of Nevada's historic mines have not been used in decades. But structures like this headframe still stand throughout the state.

Some of Nevada's mines extract lithium, which can be used in batteries.

Depression (1929–1939) hurt the US economy. This period of economic decline greatly shrunk Nevada's mining industry. There was less need for metals and other mining materials.

Government construction projects such as military bases and the Hoover Dam brought jobs and money. Gambling also brought in large amounts of money. In May 2021 casinos brought in $107 million for the state.

Even though the mining boom is over, mining remains an important industry for Nevada. The state exports more minerals than any other product. It produces more than 80 percent of the gold mined in the

United States. Nevada also mines many other minerals such as copper, gypsum, and lithium.

Nevada doesn't have much farmland. But it is able to grow crops for livestock. This helps support ranching, which is a key industry for Nevada.

Most of the rural land that is not used for farming or ranching is owned by the US government. The government owns nearly 80 percent of all land in Nevada. That is the highest percentage of any US state. The government manages this land. It uses some for military bases.

THE NEVADA TEST SITE

The US government has used Nevada's open space to test nuclear weapons. The Nevada Test Site opened in 1951 and operated until 1992. In that time, 1,021 nuclear weapons were tested. At peak operation, 125,000 people worked at the site. Today the site is open for tours. The government facility is still active, but nuclear tests are no longer done there. It is used for other kinds of nuclear research.

PERSPECTIVES

ANNIE JACOBSEN, AREA 51 EXPERT

Area 51 is a famous military base in Nevada. It is a training range for the US Air Force, but much of the base's activity is kept secret by the US government. This has led to a conspiracy theory that the base contains evidence of alien encounters. Annie Jacobsen is an author of a book about Area 51. "I have interviewed scores of very smart, very highly placed government personnel who visited the base and believe the technology they saw is so advanced that they question whether or not it's manmade," she said. "That's intriguing to me." The US government has made several statements denying the alien conspiracy theory.

It also protects some land for ranchers and for wildlife.

TOURISM

One of Nevada's biggest industries today is tourism. Casinos often have attached arenas or theaters for concerts and sporting events. There are malls for shopping. Hotels and resorts offer spas and pools to enjoy the desert sun. These attractions have made Las Vegas a world destination.

Reno is a popular tourist city in Nevada.

People also travel to Nevada's other large cities such as Reno to gamble and see shows. The state's capital, Carson City, experienced a growth in tourism in the 2010s. It is an important commercial city for northwestern Nevada. But Las Vegas is the top draw in the state. More than 42 million people visit each year. The tourism industry is worth $57 billion in Las Vegas alone.

CHAPTER
FIVE

PEOPLE AND PLACES

For nearly 100 years, Nevada has been one of the fastest-growing states. Fewer than 100,000 people lived in Nevada in 1930. Today the population is more than 3 million.

Only one in four Nevadans were born in Nevada. That has given the state a large mix of cultures. Approximately 50 percent of Nevadans are non-Hispanic white. Almost 30 percent are Hispanic or Latino.

Latino dancers celebrated their heritage at Fiesta Las Vegas in 2013.

And 10 percent are Black. Nevada also has 32 American Indian reservations.

Nevada's Hispanic population has grown quickly in the 2000s. This is in part due to an increasing number of immigrants from Mexico and countries in Central and South America. These immigrants continue their cultural and religious traditions in Nevada. One such festival is Día de los Muertos, which translates to Day of the Dead. This is a Mexican holiday that is celebrated the first two days of November. Other Hispanic cultures are also celebrated through food, music, and dances.

Each American Indian nation in Nevada celebrates its own unique culture. Some nations host annual powwows that are open to the public. These powwows preserve American Indian traditions and games. They also allow people of different backgrounds to learn more about the nation's culture. American Indian nations also celebrate their histories through arts and dance.

In 2014 the Las Vegas Paiute Tribe hosted its twenty-fifth annual powwow to celebrate American Indian cultures.

PLACES AND ACTIVITIES

Tourists come to Nevada for gambling and entertainment. Much of this is located along the Las Vegas Strip. This 4.2-mile (6.8 km) stretch of Las Vegas Boulevard is home to Las Vegas's most famous hotels.

Some consider Las Vegas to be the entertainment capital of the world. Visitors can enjoy acrobatic performances, magic shows, dance groups, and more in Las Vegas. Some music artists are resident performers at Las Vegas hotels and casinos. They perform concerts there instead of going on tour.

The city's growing population has added other entertainment options. Nevada got its first two professional sports teams in the 2010s. The Vegas Golden Knights joined the National Hockey League as a new team in 2017. And the Las Vegas Raiders football team moved to the city from Oakland,

PERSPECTIVES

THE MAN WHO BUILT LAS VEGAS

With just seven hotels on the Strip, Las Vegas looked very different in its early days. Big entertainers, like Frank Sinatra, helped attract visitors. In his book *Frank: The Voice*, James Kaplan writes, "Suddenly in this two-horse town, Sinatra meant excitement, excitement meant crowds, crowds meant gambling, and gambling meant money for the casinos. . . . In a very real way, Sinatra built Vegas: not only was he present at the creation, he was responsible for it."

Tomas Tatar celebrates after a teammate scores during Game 5 of the Stanley Cup Finals in 2018.

California, in 2020. Las Vegas has also produced many famous athletes, such as baseball All-Star Bryce Harper.

But there are lots of other activities for Nevadans to enjoy. Nevada is home to Great Basin National Park. And it shares national parks such as Lake Mead and Death Valley with Arizona and California. Nevada also has more than 20 state parks. Visitors can enjoy hiking, boating, climbing, and more.

Nevada has plenty of open space in the desert. Nevadans enjoy driving off-road vehicles such as dune buggies and all-terrain vehicles. Besides desert activities, people can also go skiing up in the mountains.

Whether originally from the state or not, Nevadans take pride in their home. It is a state that grew out of the desert. Today it is a place millions of people come to enjoy!

BURNING MAN

The Black Rock Desert in northeastern Nevada is not a place most people would live. It is flat, hot, and dry. But once a year, tens of thousands of people gather there and form a city. The Burning Man festival is designed for participants to come together with nature and each other. The festival's name comes from the huge wooden figure that is burned at the end of the event. Burning Man has been held in Nevada since 1990.

STRAIGHT TO THE
SOURCE

Growing up in Las Vegas may seem exciting. The lights and entertainment make it appear like a constant hub of action. But for people who grow up there, it is normal. Taylor Erling describes growing up in Las Vegas:

> Growing up in Las Vegas wasn't like living on Mars. . . . It was normal to me. I went to the movies (granted most movie theaters are in hotels, so that's a little weird) . . . and had sleepovers with my best friend a few blocks over.
>
> It's always hard to answer the question, "What was it like growing up in Las Vegas?" because it's a mix of a lot of things. . . . For me, growing up in Las Vegas was a little boring, over-stimulating, and normal. Growing up in my hometown was like you growing up in your hometown. Las Vegas is home.
>
> Source: Taylor Erling. "Raised in Sin City: What It's Like to Grow Up in Las Vegas." *Odyssey*, 2 Nov. 2015, theodysseyonline.com. Accessed 3 Feb. 2021.

WHAT'S THE BIG IDEA?

Take a close look at this passage. What point is the author making about growing up in Las Vegas? What connection is she making with growing up in other places?

IMPORTANT DATES

18,000 BCE
Early peoples begin living in the Nevada region.

1770s CE
The first European to visit Nevada, Francisco Garces, explores the region.

1859
Silver is discovered in Nevada, prompting people to move to the area.

1864
Nevada is admitted as the thirty-sixth state in the United States on October 31, despite its very low population.

1878
Nevada's mining industry reaches peak silver production, putting out what would be worth $1 billion today.

1914
Women in Nevada gain the right to vote six years ahead of women living in other areas of the United States.

1931
Nevada legalizes gambling.

1933
Construction begins on the Hoover Dam on June 6.

2018
Nevada's population tops 3 million, the result of decades as one of the fastest-growing states in the country.

STOP AND THINK

Tell the Tale

Chapter Two of this book discusses the discovery of silver in Nevada. Imagine you had discovered this precious metal in the state. Write 200 words about your big discovery. Would you sell the silver or keep it? What would you do with the money?

Surprise Me

Chapter Three discusses the geography of Nevada. After reading this book, what two or three facts about Nevada's geography did you find most surprising? Write a few sentences about each fact. Why did you find each fact surprising?

Why Do I Care?

Maybe you do not live in Nevada. But that doesn't mean you can't think about how climate change affects the state. Do you have friends or family who live in desert areas? How would worrying about droughts and wildfires affect your life?

Take a Stand

Some people come to Nevada to see the sights of Las Vegas. Others enjoy the outdoor activities. Which Nevada activity would you most like to take part in? Why?

GLOSSARY

adaptation
a feature or skill that helps an animal or plant survive

depression
a period of time when the economy struggles, usually causing job loss

discrimination
when people treat others differently based on certain factors such as appearance

economy
a place's system of goods, services, money, and jobs

gamble
to bet money or other stakes on a game of chance or on the way a game, race, or other event will end

immigrant
a person who moves to and lives in a new country

livestock
animals that farmers raise for food, labor, or products

reservation
an area of land set aside for American Indian peoples

ONLINE RESOURCES

To learn more about Nevada, visit our free resource websites below.

Visit **abdocorelibrary.com** or scan this QR code for free Common Core resources for teachers and students, including vetted activities, multimedia, and booklinks, for deeper subject comprehension.

Visit **abdobooklinks.com** or scan this QR code for free additional online weblinks for further learning. These links are routinely monitored and updated to provide the most current information available.

LEARN MORE

Bassier, Emma. *Minerals*. Abdo, 2020.

Manzanero, Paula K. *Where Is Area 51?* Penguin, 2018.

Ryan, Todd. *Las Vegas Raiders*. Abdo, 2020.

INDEX

American Civil War, 6, 15
Area 51, 32

Boundary Peak, 7, 22

cacti, 26–27
Carson City, 7, 17, 33
Colorado River, 7, 19, 22, 24

deserts, 7, 8, 12, 17, 21, 24–26, 32, 40

gambling, 6, 18, 30, 33, 37, 38
Garces, Francisco, 13
Great Basin, 8, 11, 21–22, 39

Hispanic population, 35–36
Hoover Dam, 7, 19, 30

Lake Mead, 7, 19, 25, 39
Lake Tahoe, 7, 13, 22
Las Vegas, 5–6, 7, 8, 12, 16, 18, 22, 24–25, 32–33, 37–39, 41

military, 30–31, 32
mining, 29–31

nuclear research, 31

Paiute, 11–12, 14
Paleo-Indians, 11
Pyramid Lake, 7, 12, 26–27

Reno, 6, 7, 8, 18, 33

sagebrush, 17, 26
Shoshone, 11, 13
Sierra Nevada, 13, 22
silver, 5, 15, 17, 29
Sinatra, Frank, 38
sports, 32, 38–39

tourism, 6, 8, 19, 32–33, 37

Wašiw, 11, 13
Winnemucca, Sarah, 14

About the Author

Richard Sebra is a children's book author and journalist. He and his wife enjoy cooking, surfing, and hiking with their dogs.